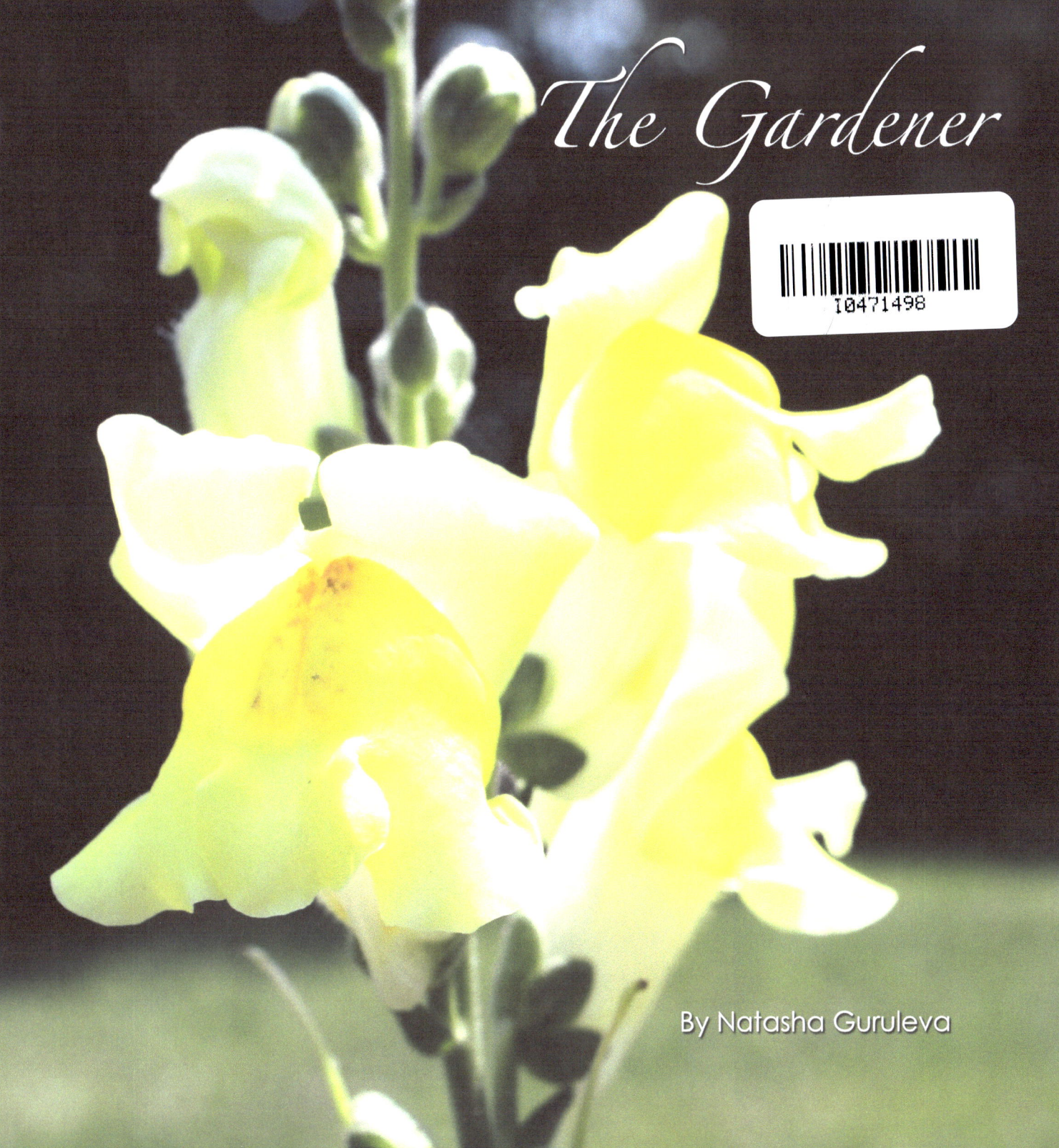

The Gardener

By Natasha Guruleva

To Dale

GARDENER

The flowers reign over the green alley of the garden,
their bright colors dominate the landscape,
their subdued colors emphasize the dominance of the bright ones.
Exquisite shapes reach perfection through the years of selection,
their fragrance manifests their being for the ones whose eyes are closed;
their purity and resilience inspire imagination and thoughts of loftier nature.
But I think about a gardener, whose work is hard,
whose heart is humble, whose presence is unnoticeable.

Like a pearl diver
who can't claim the authorship over a gorgeous pearl jewelry,
displayed in a store,
though he's the one who found and pulled the pearl out of a mollusk
lying on the bottom of a sea;
like a miner who first discovers crystal clusters,
growing in the darkness of a mine,
and brings them to shine under the beams of daylight,
grateful just for witnessing the wonder,

the gardener can't put his name on the petals of flowers he grows,
nor does he feel a creator
though he puts his heart and soul
in helping plants develop into gorgeous blooms.
He is an anonymous protector, a faithful guardian.
he rejoices in colors and shapes of pure beauty,
his red blood mixes with green juices of stems
and becomes brown tan on his tired hands.
He speaks plant's tongue and sings their song,
accompanied by rapture, he silences his soul in their peace.

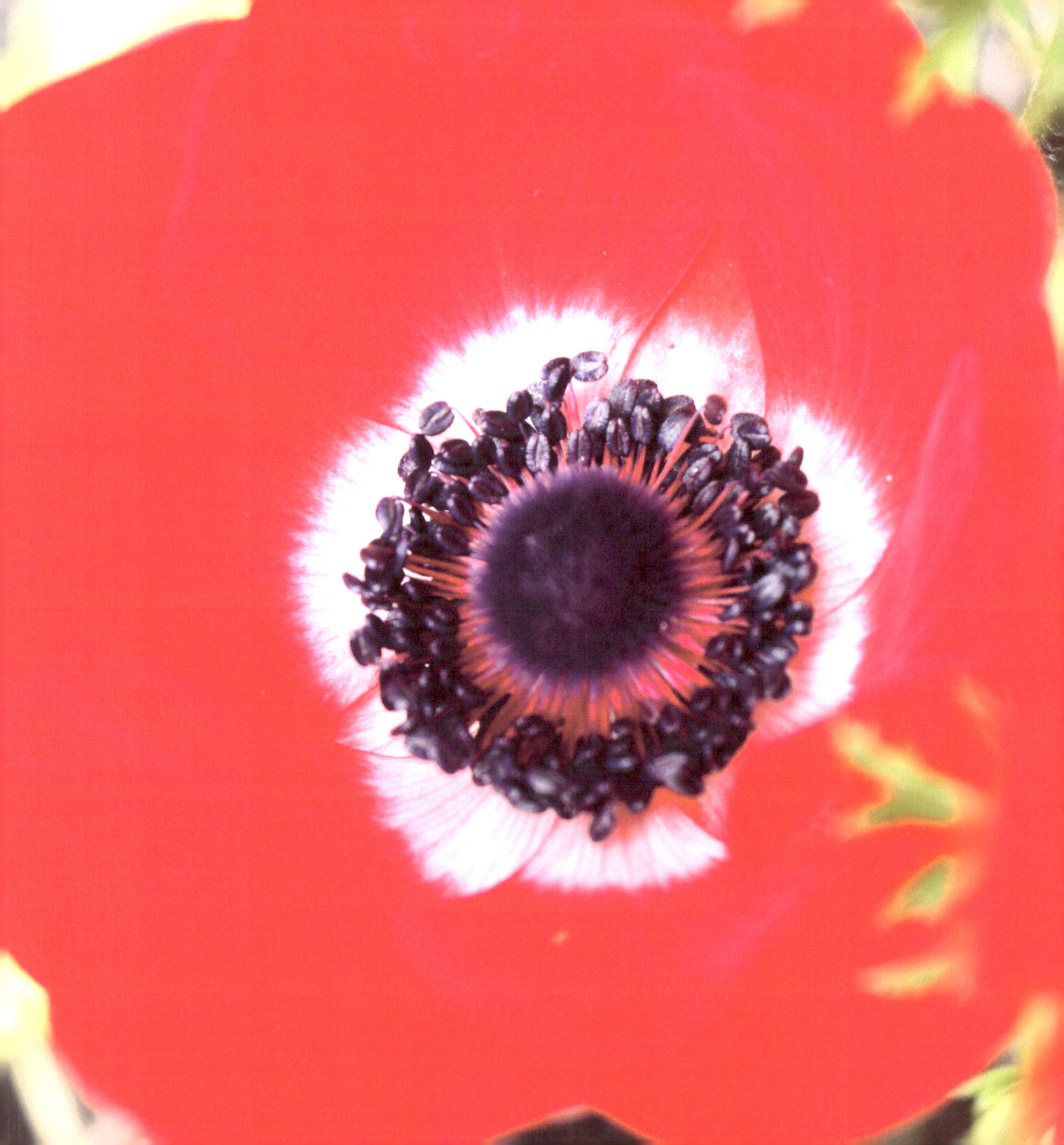

RED

silent moan
of ecstasy
is palpable in the air.
Trembling with excitement,
flashing its red of desire,
humble stem
carries his fragile bloom
that sings
a song of love.

AMARYLLIS

A foreign prince

in all his grandeur

proudly presents his being

to the dwellers of the garden.

He expects

to be awed

and admired.

He is not aware

of treacherous trials

of storms and cold

awaiting him

in this hostile land.

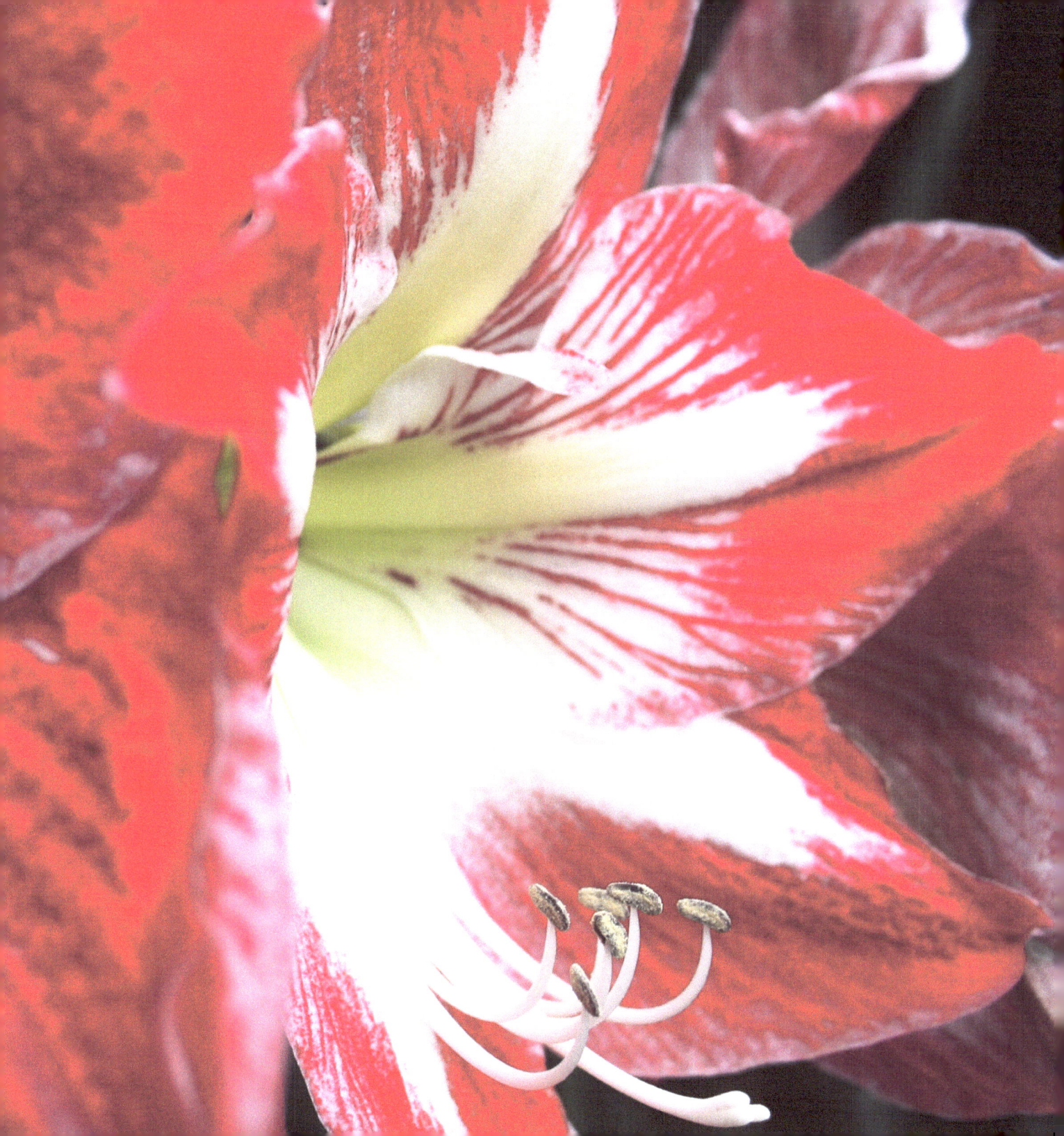

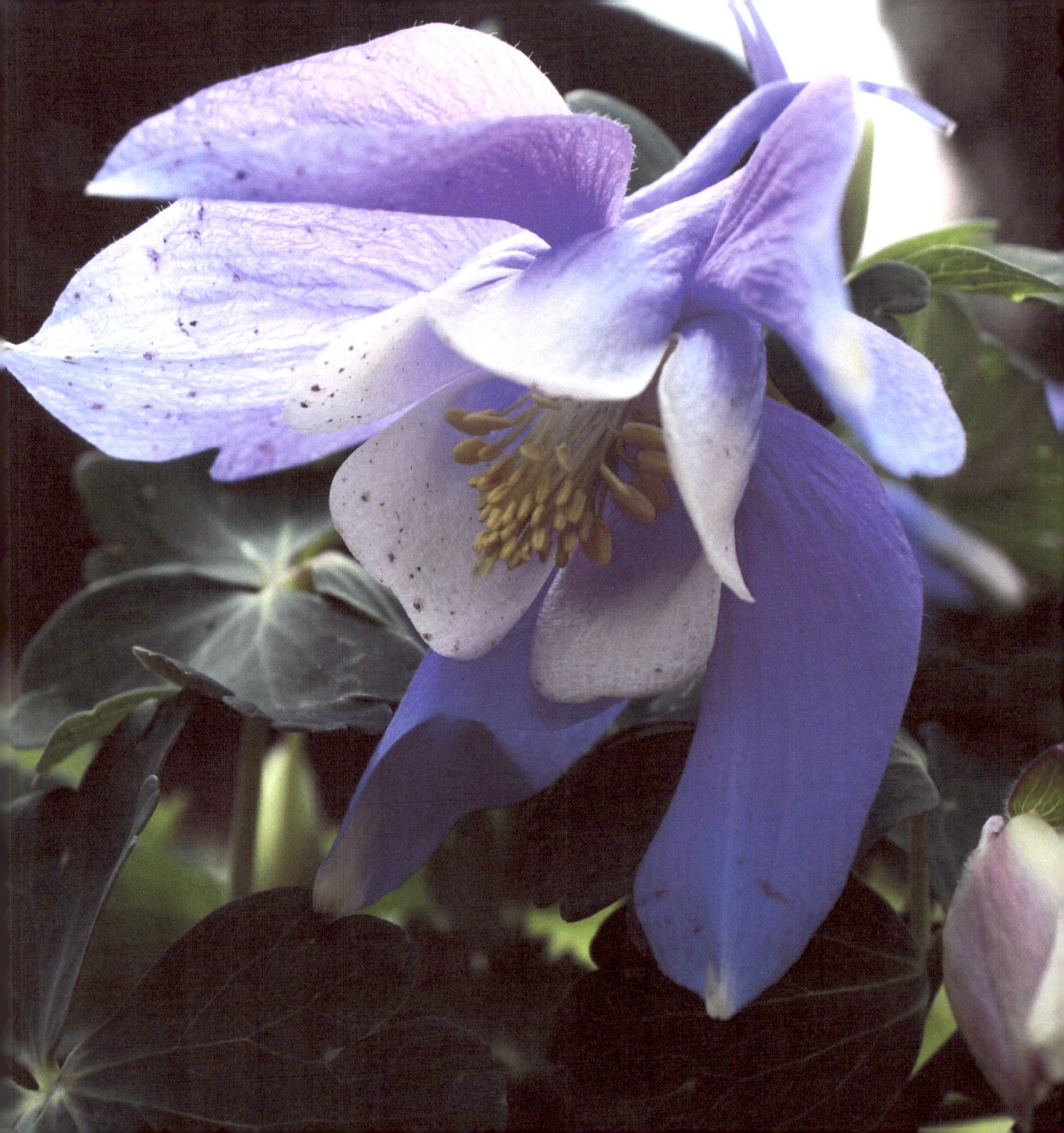

COLUMBINES

Laughing quietly
they perform on the green arena
under the bright spotlight of sun,
juggling with the droplets
of spring rain,
making funny faces
at the other flowers
that didn't come to bloom
just yet,
bowing to the ones
that blossom
when the curtain
of shade dims the light.

BELL

Amidst the boisterous dance
of verdure,
the feast of colors

and smells,
you call for silence,
you summon quietness,
you ask to listen,
you pursue attention,
you convey rest.

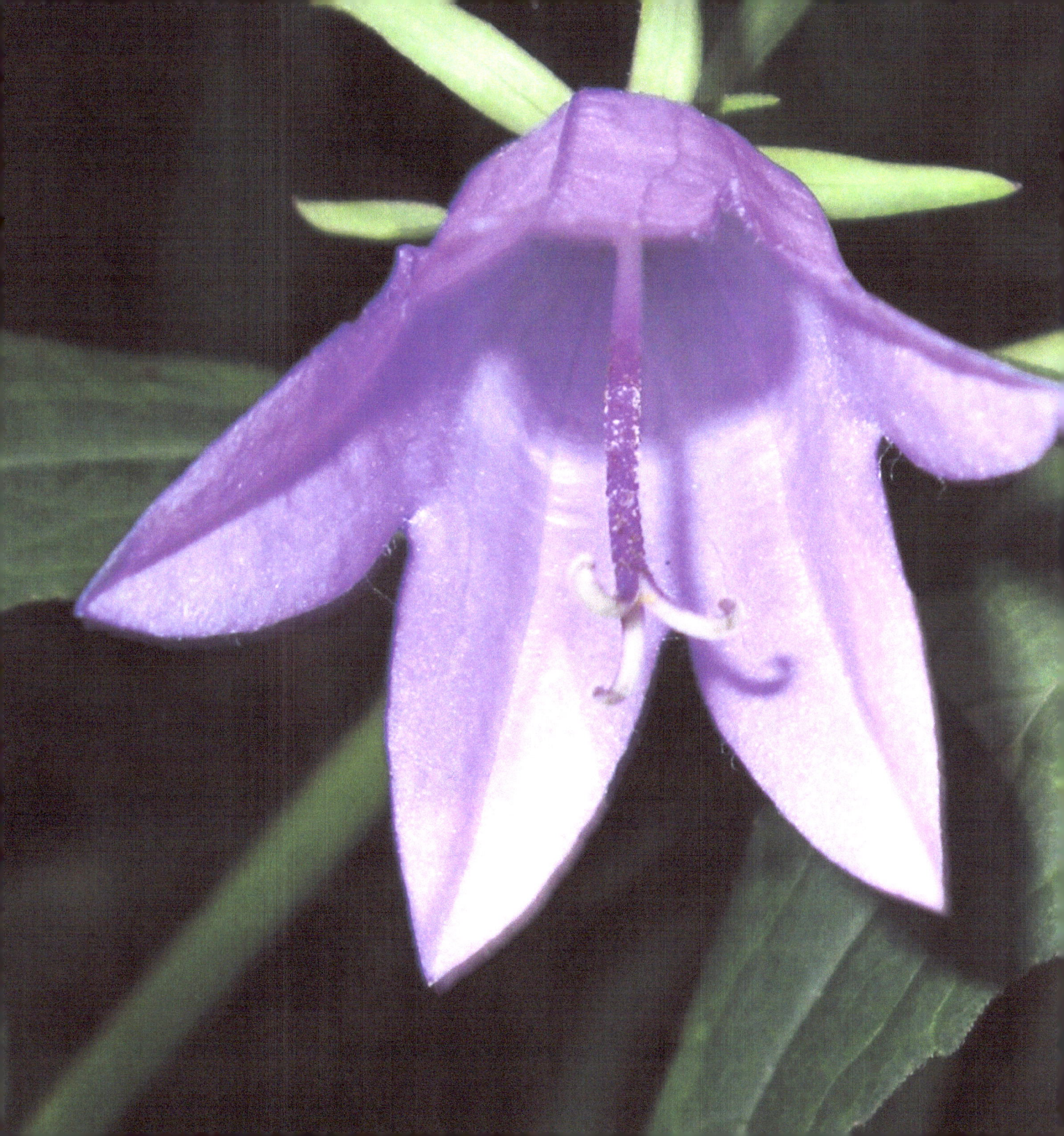

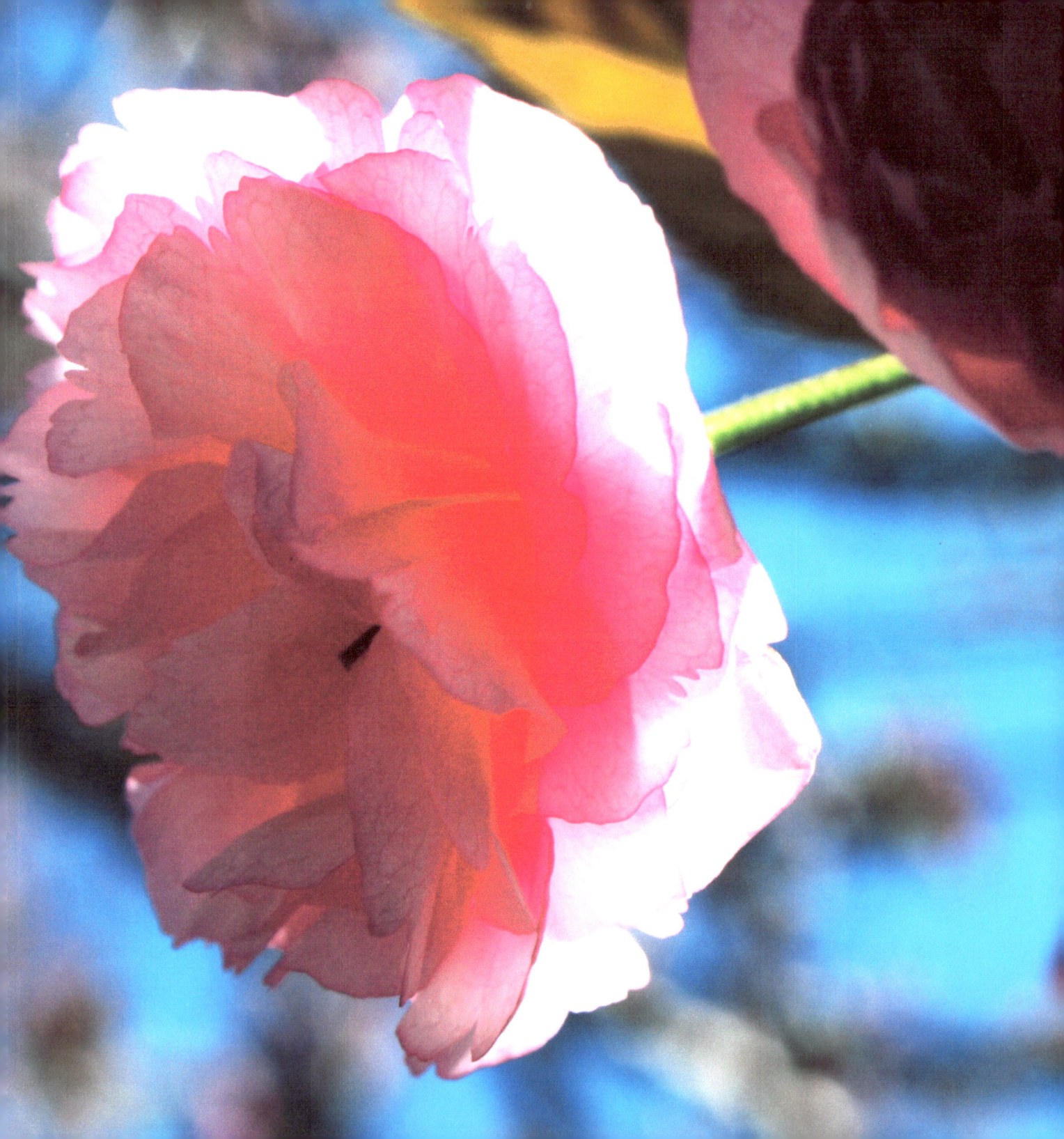

PINK

I don't like pink. I wish I could avoid it.

Life teaches me not only the tolerance

but love of what I don't like.

I didn't like red-haired boys.

Ironically, men who became so dear to me have red hair.

I didn't like orange cats and dogs, but the feline being I adore is orange.

I didn't like ineloquent people, and one of them I married.

I didn't like big cities and crowds,

and I live in one of the biggest cities in the world,

where the density of population is over

sixty nine thousand per squire mile. I didn't like small apartments,

and I live in the squalor of my flat in Manhattan.

Every spring the tree that roots on the neighbors' property,

spreads its branches, thickly covered with blossoms, over our yard.

It's impossible to avoid or not to love these blooms.

They are pink.

CHRYSANTHEMUM

I get drunk
from this bitter-sweet aroma.
The smell is unassuming,
yet powerful.
It always keeps royal blooms
under the spell of memory
of their humble beginnings:
the fine fragrance
of aristocracy
and gracious beauty
blends
with the hard sweat
of a gardener.

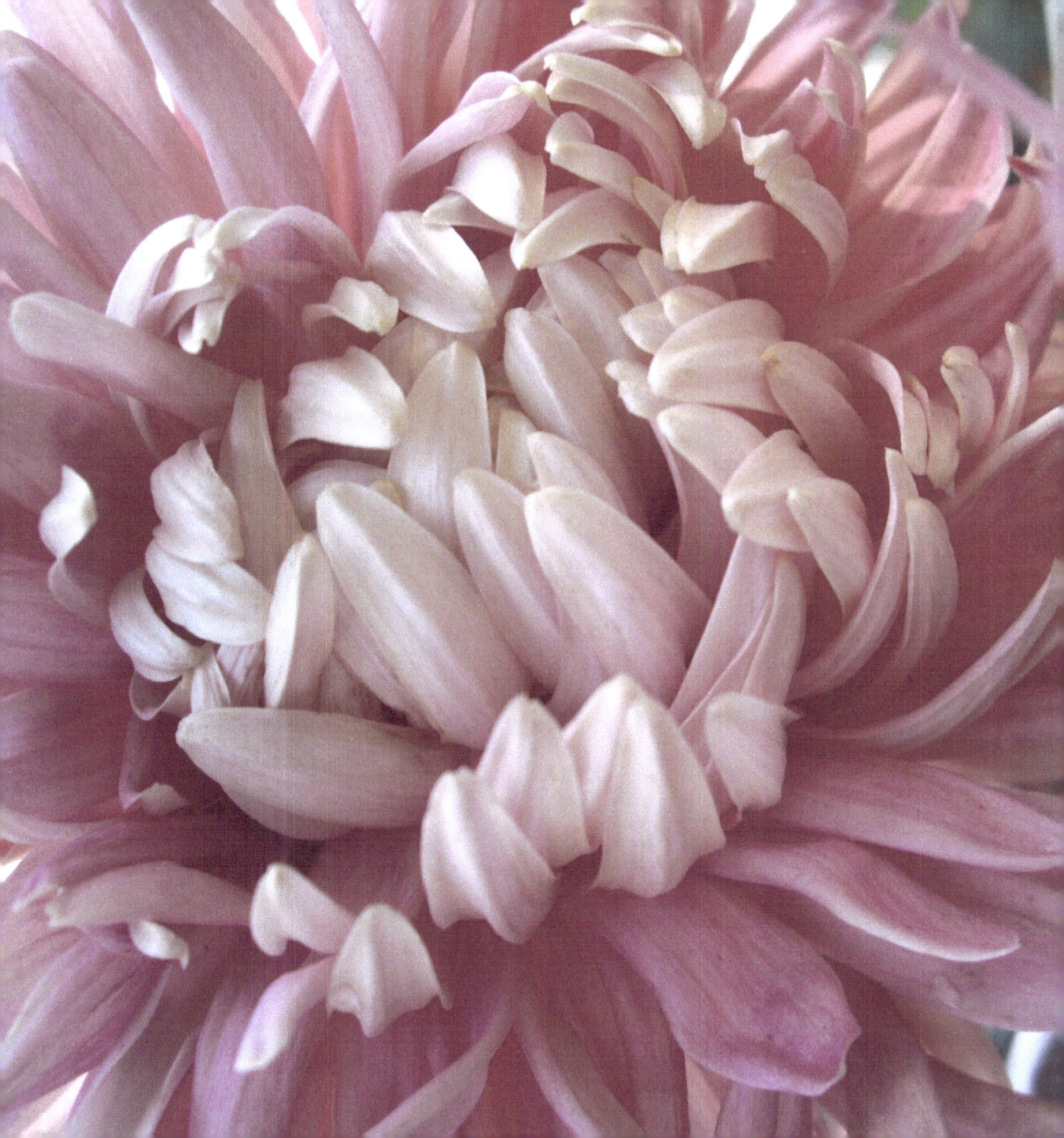

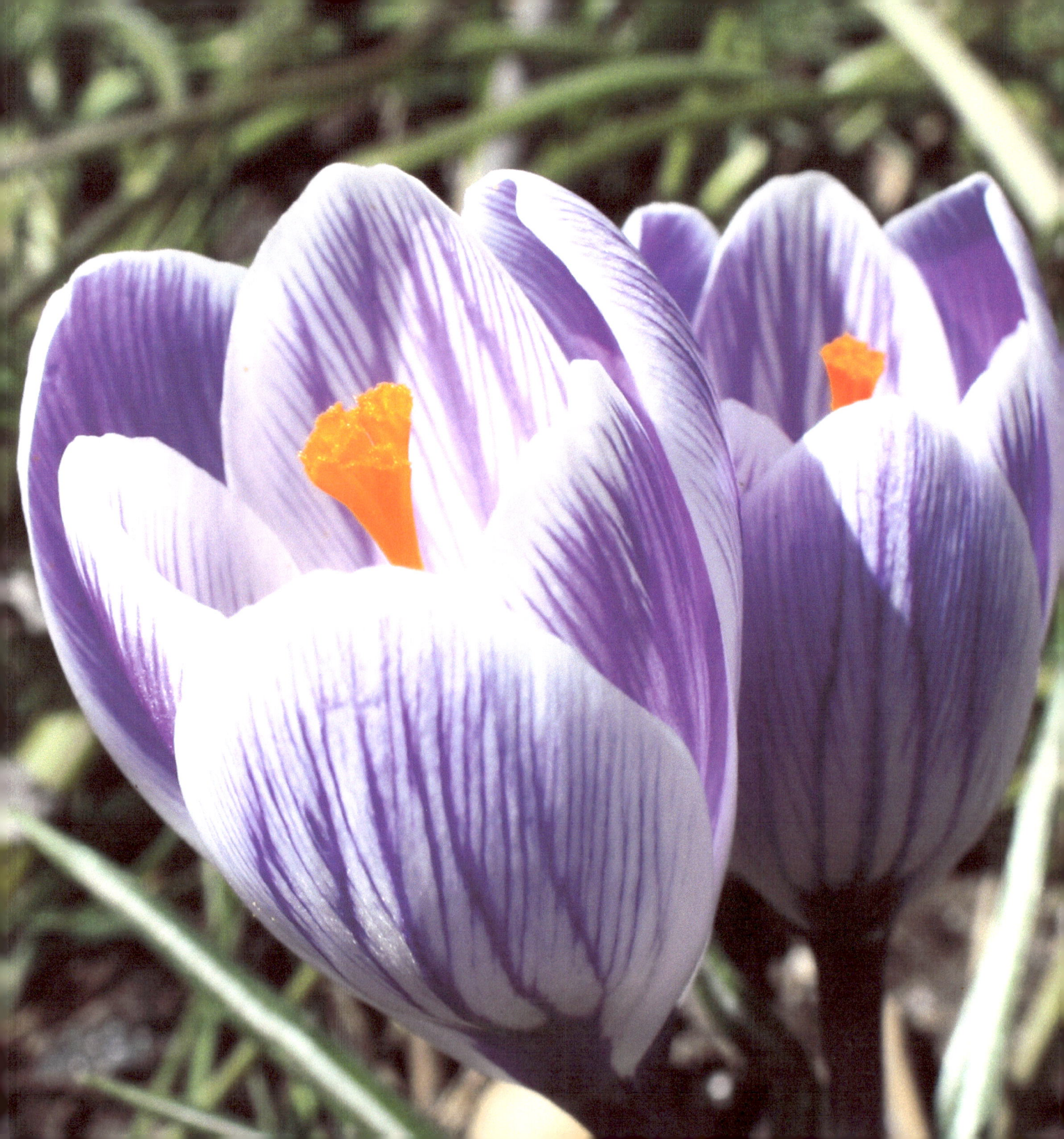

MESSENGERS

While the earth
is bare – waking up,
licking her winter wounds,
healing frostbites
with rivulets
of thawing snow;
the first messengers
of spring
pierce the cold soil
and deliver
summons
of life.

GARDENER'S PRAYER

Let me blend with the dirt -

so I could hear the heartbeat of my mother.

Let me grow as free and simple as grass -

so I learn strength and humility.

Let me form a bud

and bear a blossom -

so I could feel the passion of eagerness

to be touched by the sun.

Let me open my bloom -

so my soul could bathe in the light

and breathe the air,

stretching its shiny beams

in greetings of the other souls.

Let me hear the song of life -

so I can sing it.

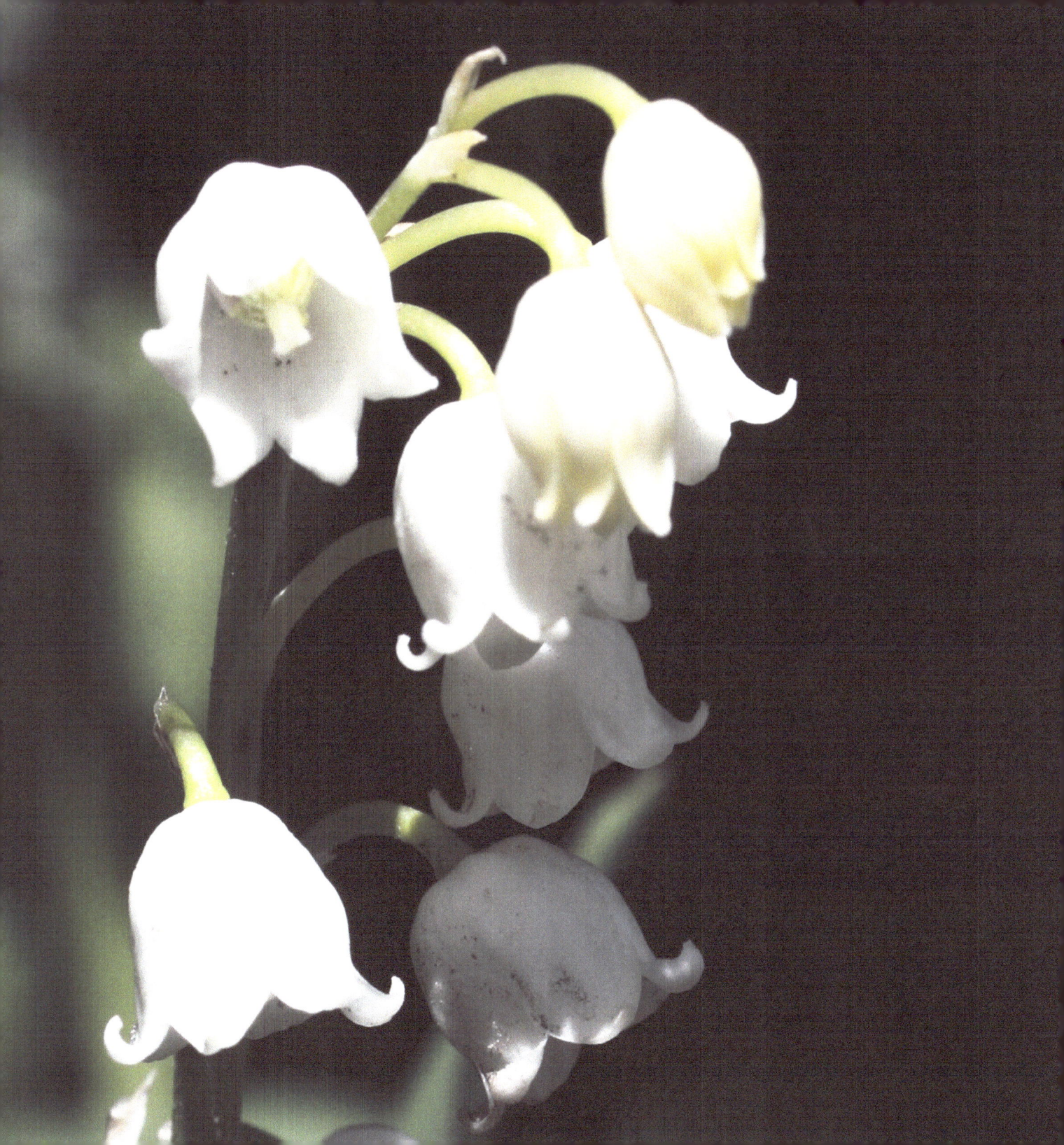

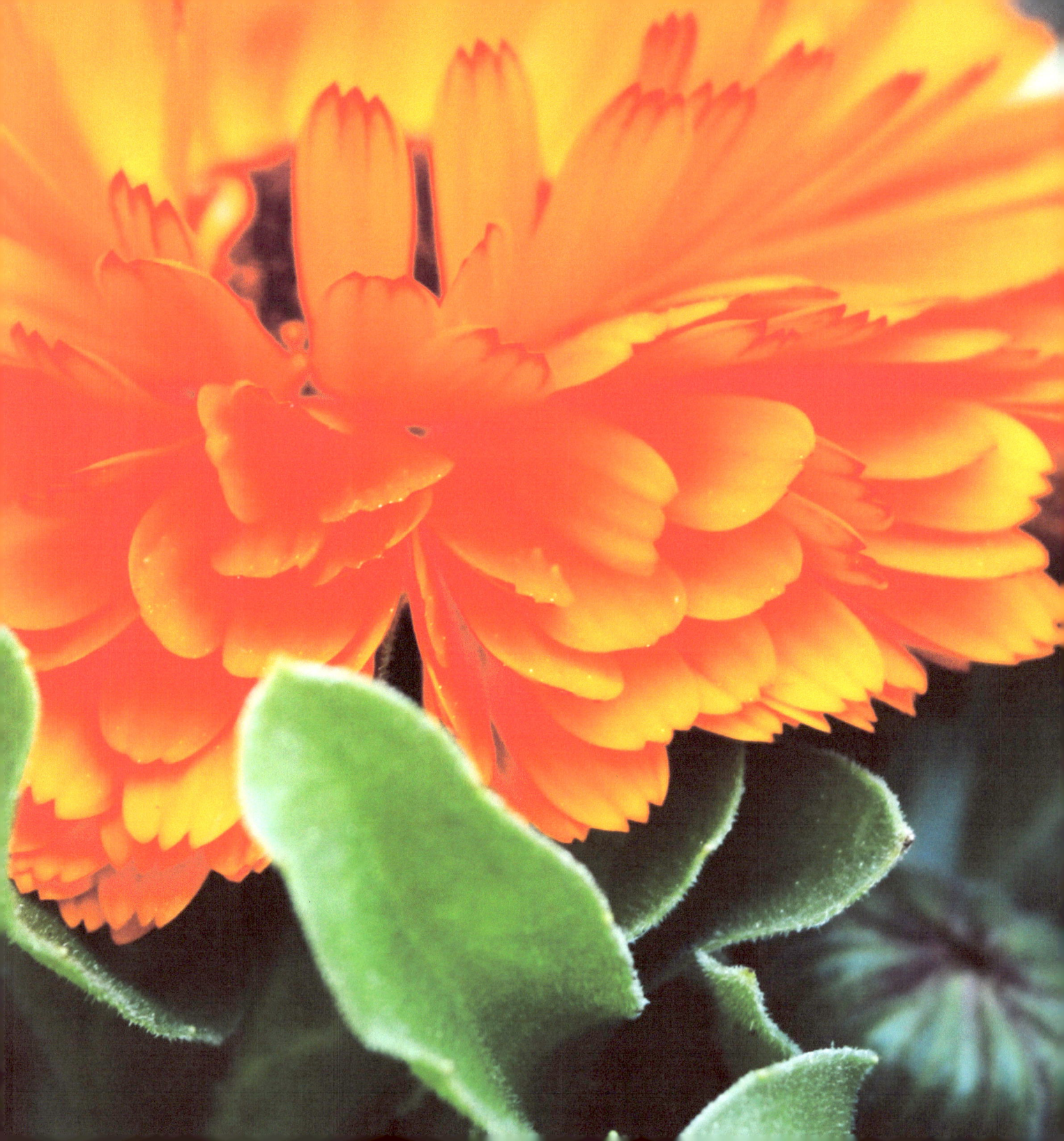

SHE LOVES ME

Gaily smiling
right into my face,
opening the feathery fan
of her petals,
she teases me,
coquettishly fending off
my admiring glance:
dare not ruin my adornments
in your perpetual
"she-loves-me-she-loves-me-not" quest.
Silly flower,
why would I trouble myself
with such labor,
if every cell of your being
says loudly:
I love you so!

ORANGE

Restless stirring

of shiny petals

tickles the sky.

It laughs in response.

The laugh is contagious,

the sun starts laughing too

and ignites the flame,

which lights up the flowers.

Their warmth caresses

grateful earth.

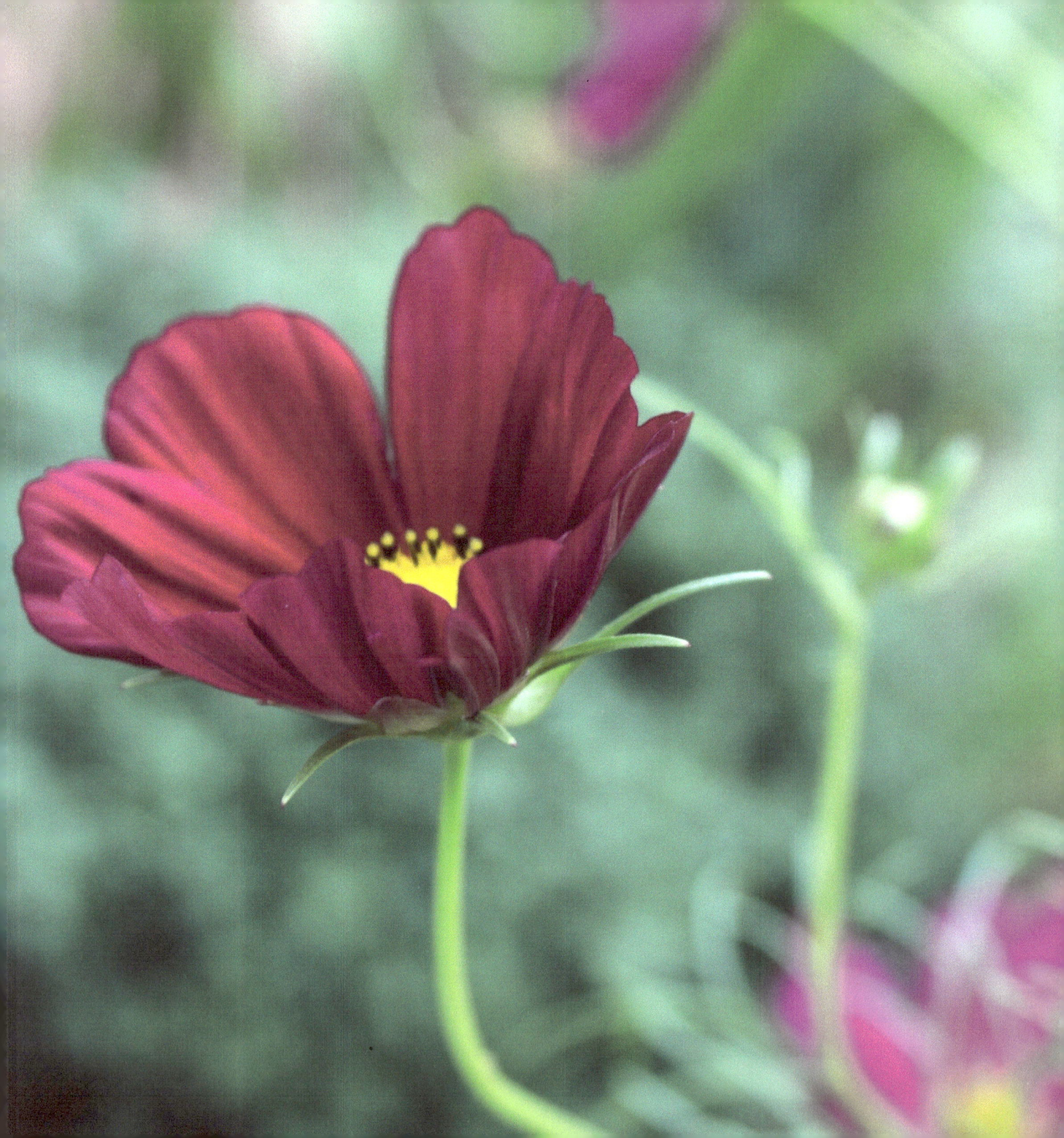

SMILE FROM FARAWAY

The petals of my childhood...
They were everywhere.
On practically every block of my city
there were flowerbeds -
large and small,
grotesque in their grandeur
and tiny spots of leftover seedlings.
Different plants grew there,
pulling their stems to the sun,
forming buds, coming to bloom,
then withering and fading.
But the star-petals of cosmea
smiled at us all the time,
without any breaks.
We, children, used to pop buds
that were ready to open
and suck their juice,
feeling unity and
throbbing eagerness of life.

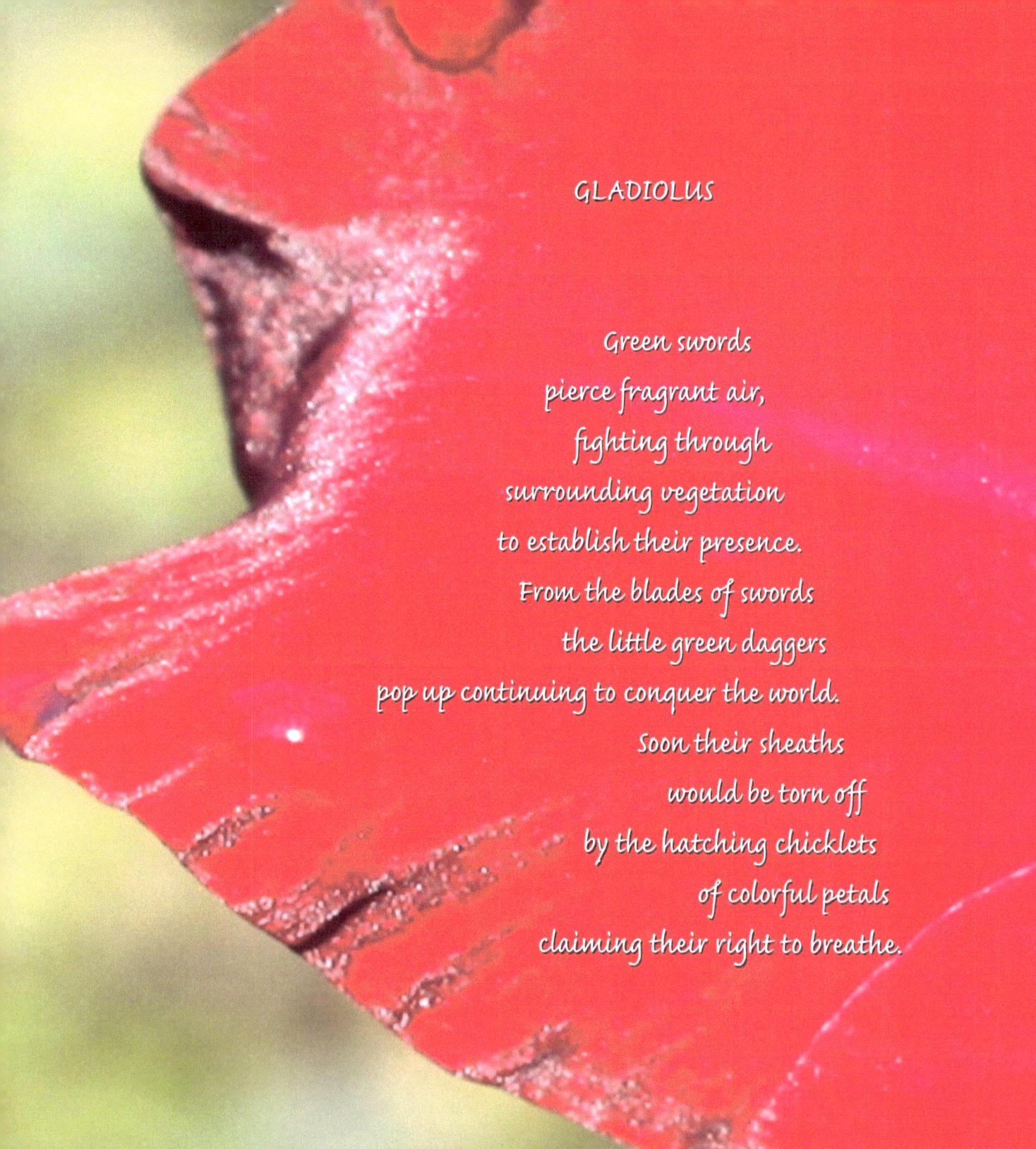

GLADIOLUS

Green swords
pierce fragrant air,
fighting through
surrounding vegetation
to establish their presence.
From the blades of swords
the little green daggers
pop up continuing to conquer the world.
Soon their sheaths
would be torn off
by the hatching chicklets
of colorful petals
claiming their right to breathe.

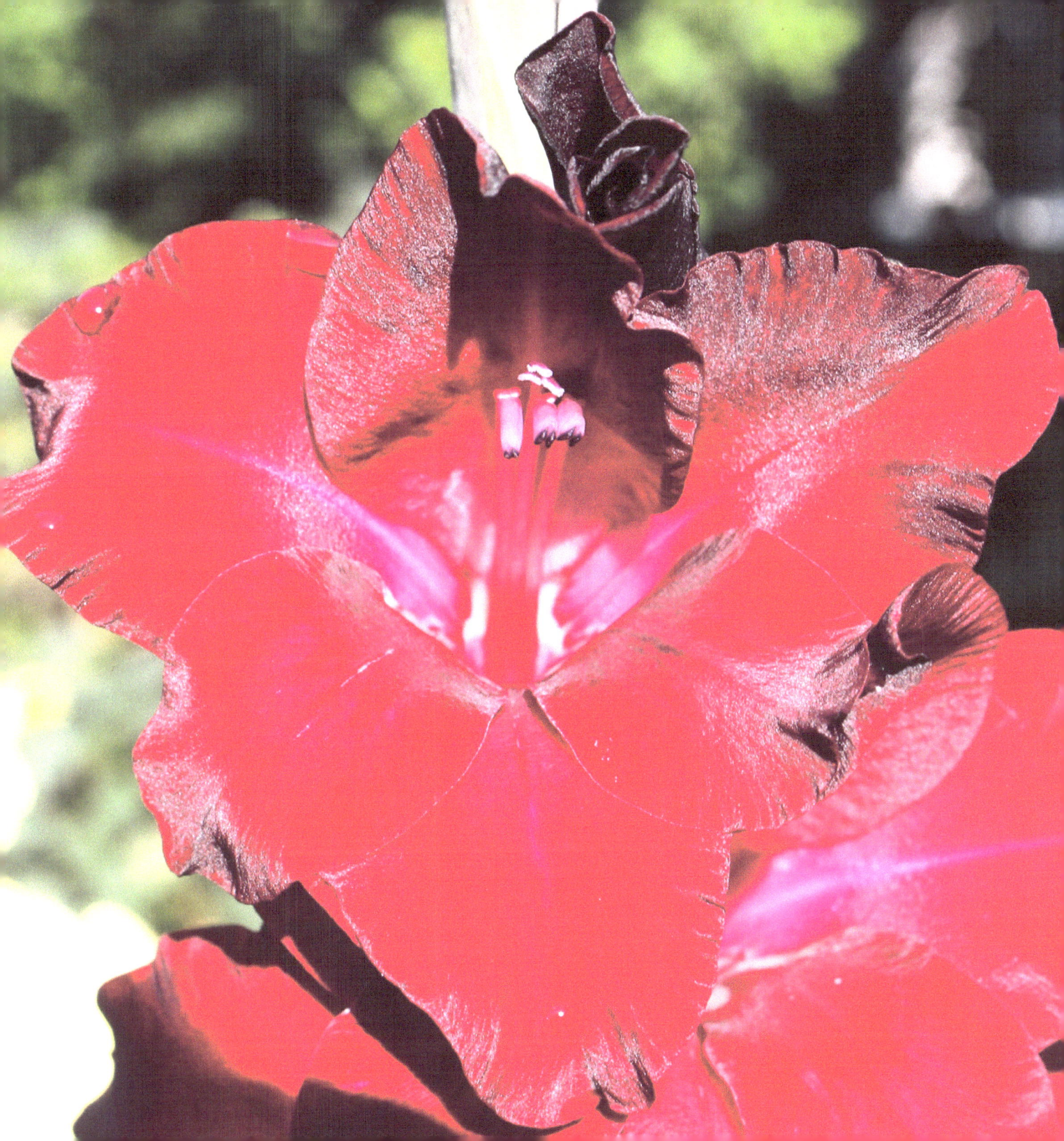

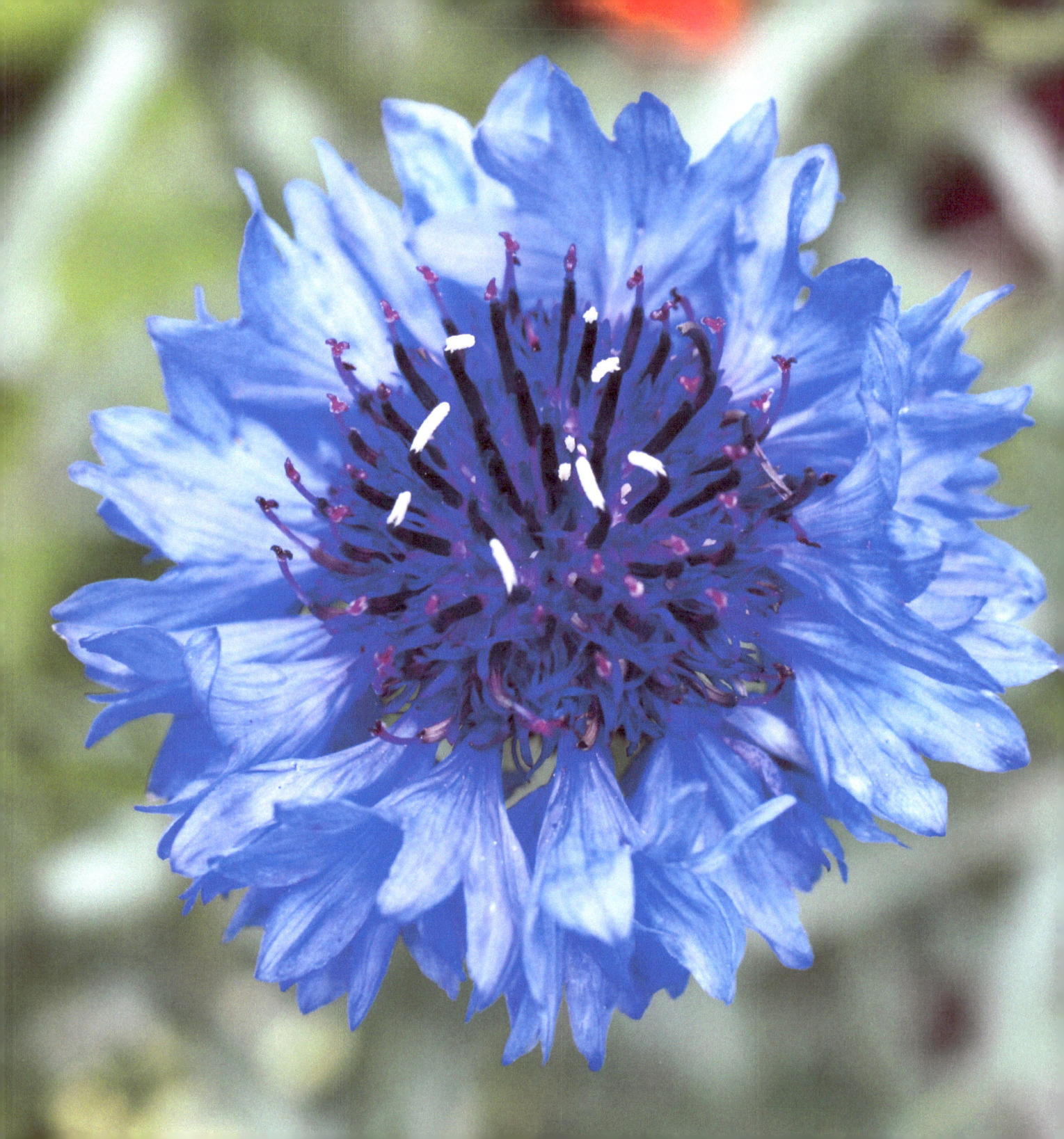

BLUE

Reflection of blue sky
Is concentrated
In small unpretentious flower.
It guards
this piece of sky
with all its strength -
flower's treasure is the only blue
in the midst of live carpet
of green and purple,
white and yellow,
red and pink,
orange and lilac.
The flower protects its only blue,
so the sky can see its reflection
and smile in joy.

I HEAR YOU

The bloom of flower

is like a sea urchin,

it lets you hear

the other world.

When I listen

to the song of clematis

I hear my mother

calling me home.

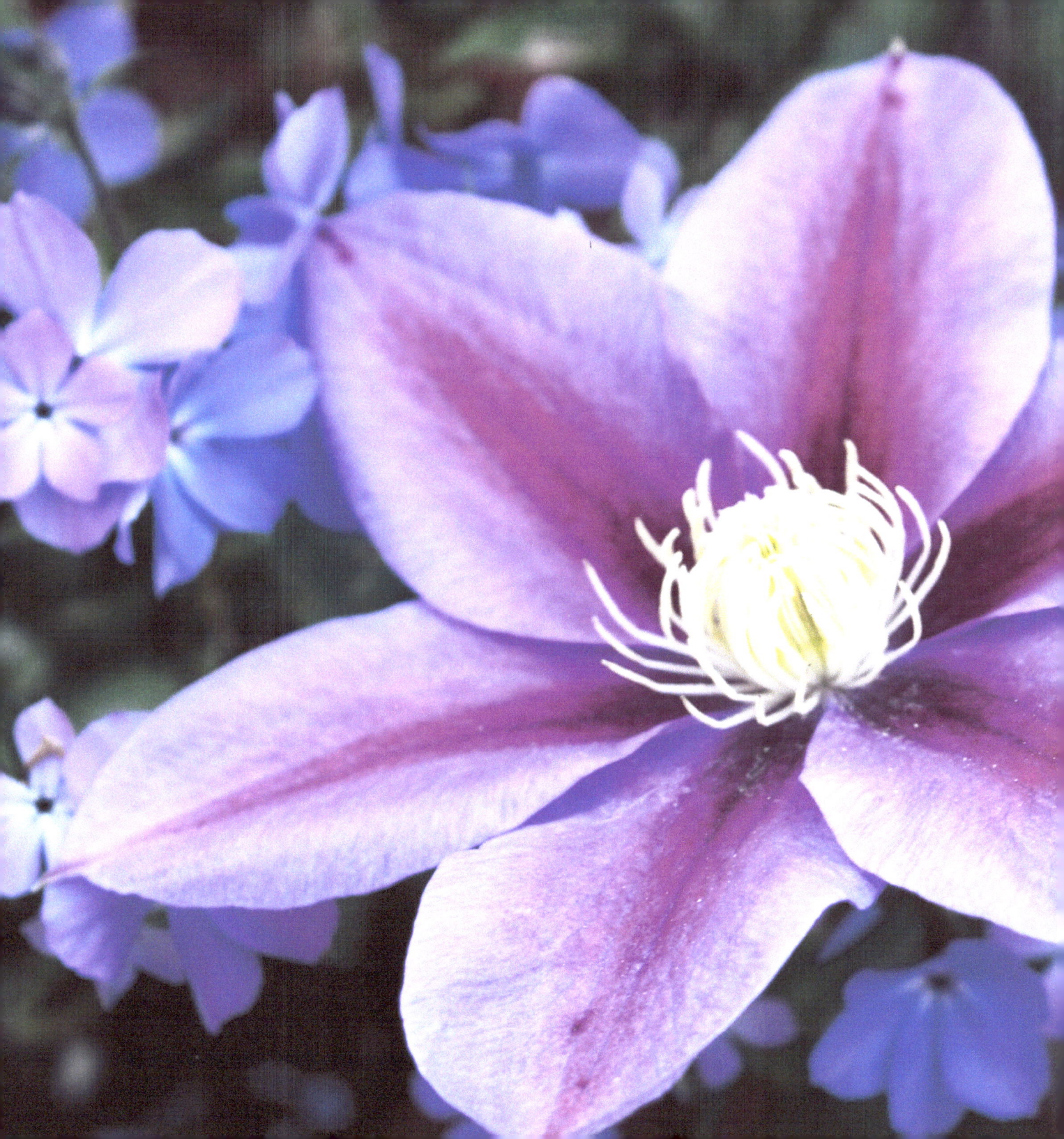

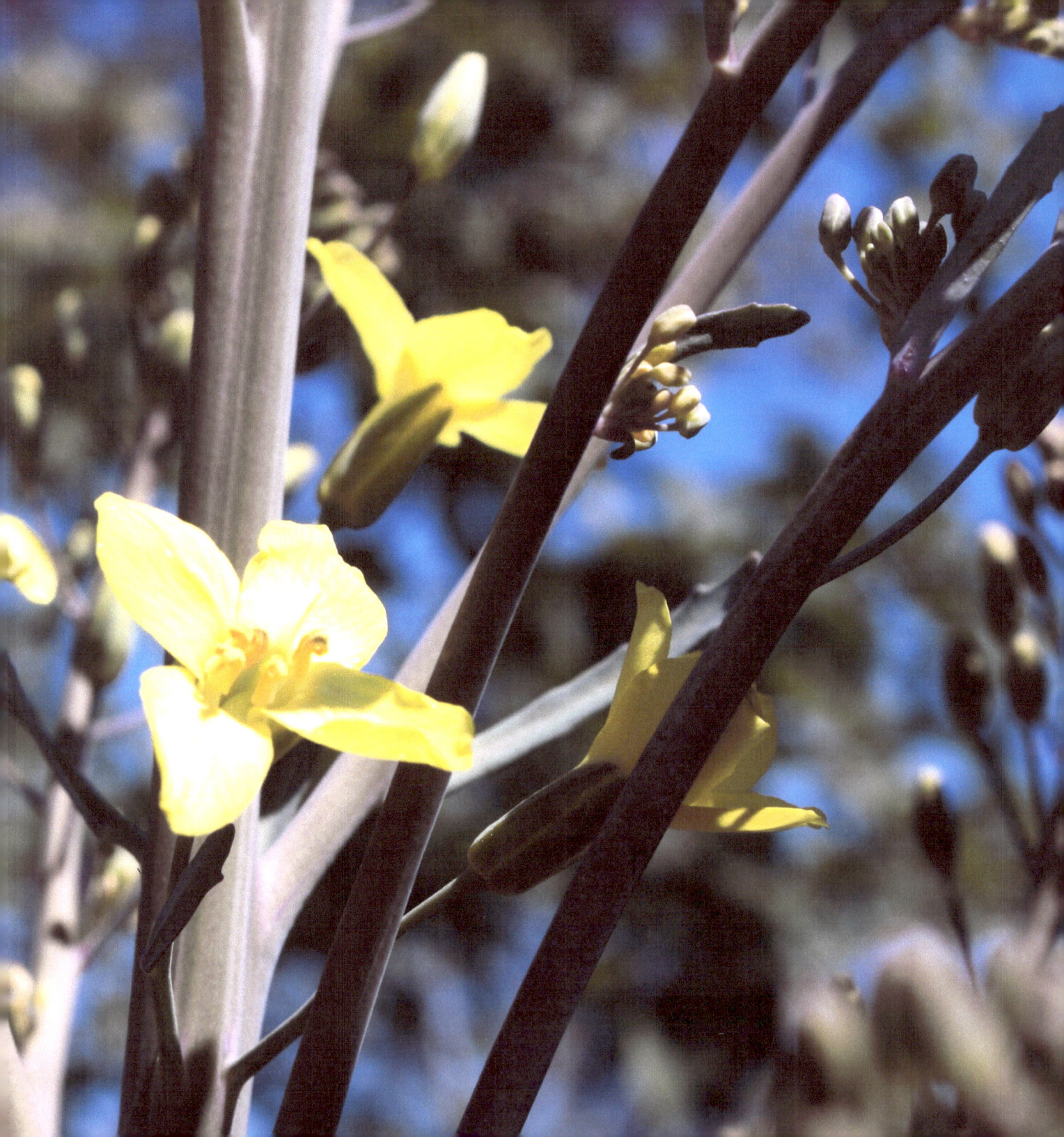

FATE

Destined to become
a vegetable,
cabbage
fights for a chance
to change its fate -
to bloom
and be a flower,
embellishing the garden
with modest
but abundant blossoms.

MIRACLE

I never get used
to this miracle:
how from a little
unpretentious seed,
survived from birds,
squirrels
and deadly sleep of winter,
such magnificent beauty
unfolds.

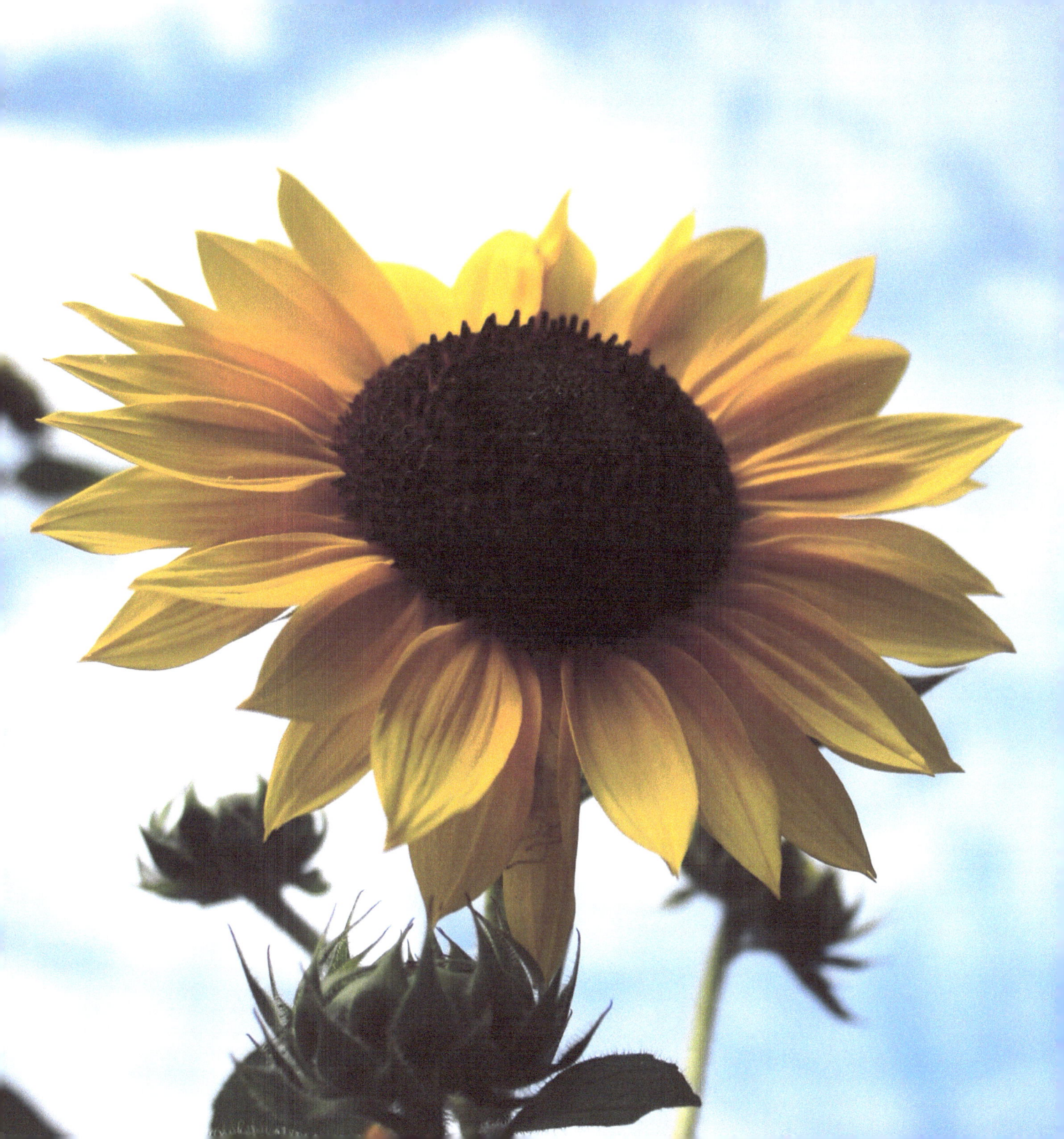

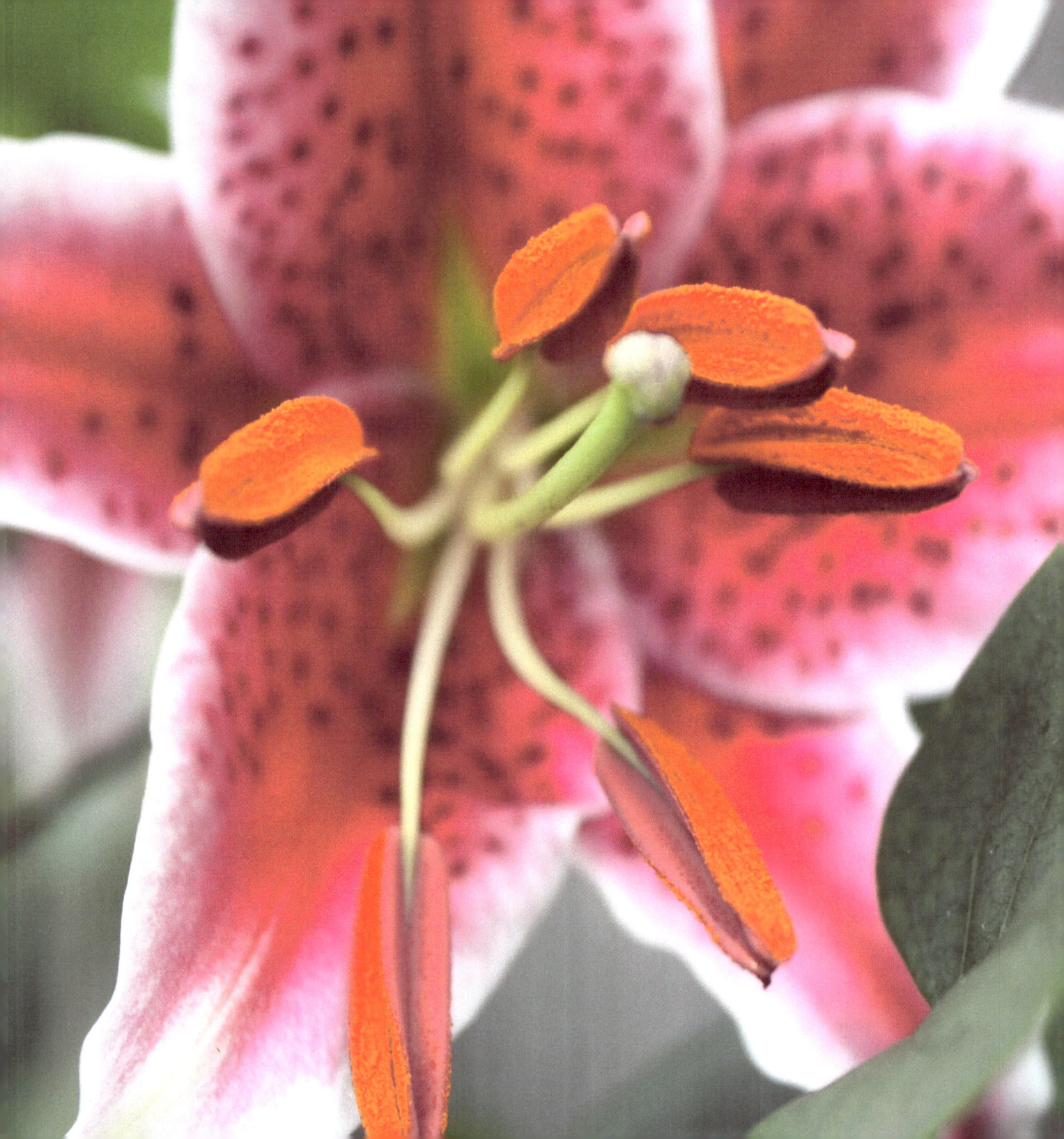

LILY

The particles
of divine aroma
enter my lungs
and give a boost
to the instrument
of my body-
the organ
starts playing.
The music excites
the tiny particles
of divine aromas
they dance
and the music
goes on and on.

A KISS FOR DAHLIA

Through the myriads of mirrors
of cold morning dew
I see reflections
of familiar friendly souls
warmly greeting me:
hi... hi... hi...
While my lips,
kissing autumn lips of Dahlia,
whisper:
bye... bye... bye...

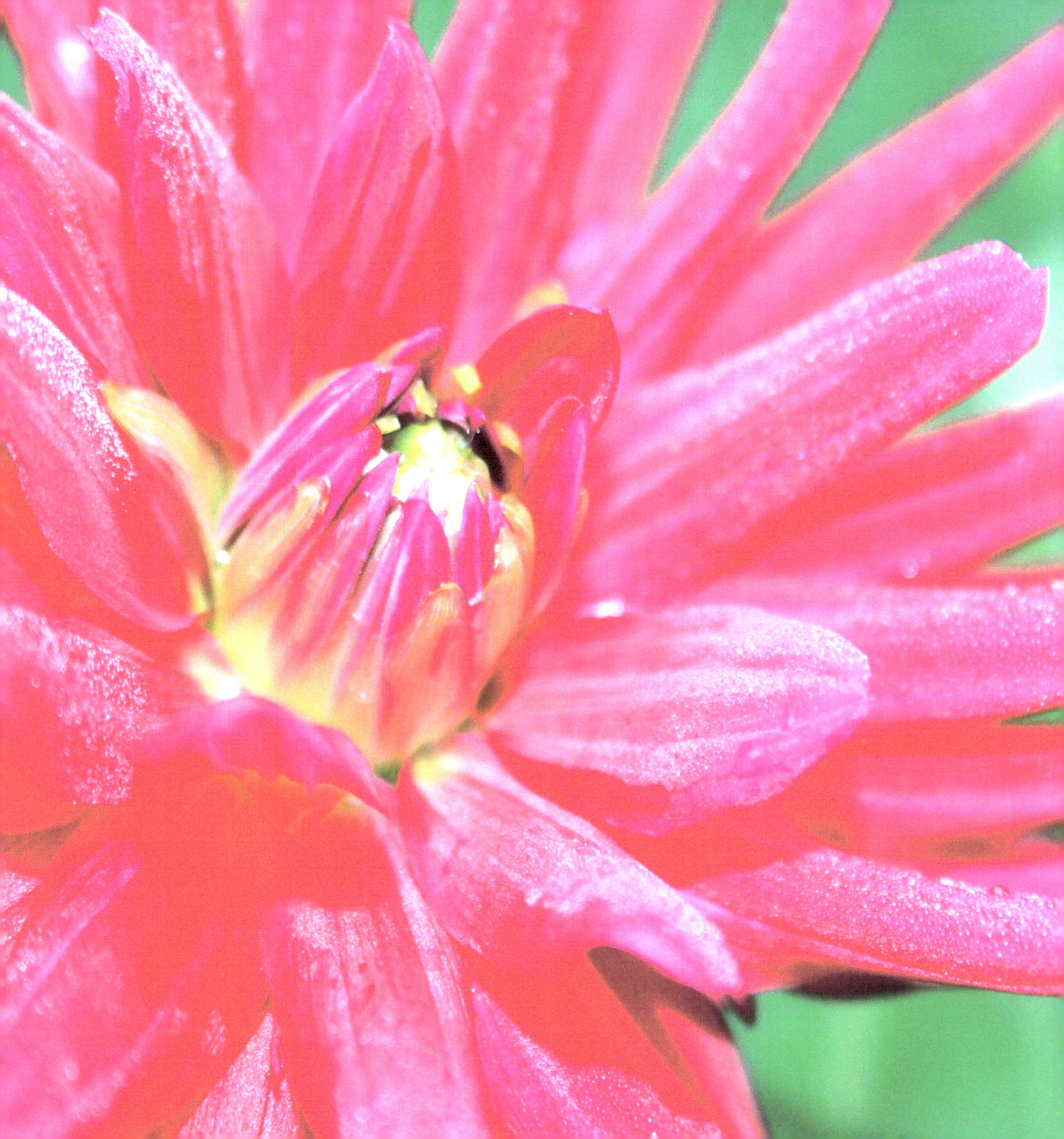

www.ingramcontent.com/pod-product-compliance
Lightning Source LLC
Chambersburg PA
CBHW051110180526
45172CB00002B/850